THAT WOMAN

THAT WOMAN

Daniel Danis

Translated by Linda Gaboriau

TALONBOOKS

1998

Talonbooks
#104—3100 Production Way
Burnaby, British Columbia, Canada V5A 4R4

Typeset in New Aster and Avant Garde and printed and bound in Canada by Hignell Printing Ltd.

First Printing: October 1998

Talonbooks are distributed in Canada by General Distribution Services, 325 Humber College Blvd., Toronto, Ontario, Canada M9W 7C3; Tel.:(416) 213-1919; Fax:(416) 213-1917.
Talonbooks are distributed in the U.S.A. by General Distribution Services Inc., 85 Rock River Drive, Suite 202, Buffalo, New York, U.S.A. 14207-2170; Tel.:1-800-805-1083; Fax:1-800-481-6207.

Celle-là was published in 1993 in the original French by Leméac Éditeur, Montréal, Québec.

CANADIAN CATALOGUING IN PUBLICATION DATA
Danis, Daniel, 1962-
  [Celle-là. English]
  That woman

  A play.
  Translation of: Celle-là.
  ISBN 0-88922-399-8

  I. Title. II. Title: Celle-là. English.
PS8557.A5667C4413 1998   C842'.54   C98-910729-9
PQ3919.2.D248C4413 1998

Celle-là was first produced in French by Espace Go
and premiered in Montreal on January 12, 1993 with
the following cast:

THE MOTHER	Isabelle Miquelon
THE OLD MAN	Marc Legault
THE SON	Jean-François Pichette

Directed by Louise Laprade
Assisted by Sabrina Steenhaut
Set design by Stéphane Roy
Costume design by François Barbeau
Lighting design by Michel Beaulieu
Music by Vincent Beaulne

That Woman was first produced in English by Theatre Cryptic in Glasgow, and premiered at the Edinburgh Festival on August 9, 1997 with the following cast:

THE MOTHER   Kathryn Akin, actor,
                  & Marianne Cotterill, soprano
THE OLD MAN   Steven Beard, actor,
                  & Richard Burkhard, baritone
THE SON   Stéphane Théoret

Directed by Cathy Boyd
Assisted by Stéphane Théoret
Production design by Alex Rigg
Lighting design by Stewart Steel
Music composed by Anthea Haddow & Jenny Scott
Music performed by
Anthea Haddow, cellist, & Jenny Scott, clarinettist

The English translation was first workshopped at the Banff Playwrights' Colony in June 1994 under the direction of Kim McCaw.

CHARACTERS

THE MOTHER, a woman either twenty-eight or
fifty-nine years old.

THE OLD MAN, a man of sixty-nine.

THE SON, a man of thirty-one.

PLACE

Rented flat in a provincial town. All three characters
remain in the flat until the Mother's departure.

TIME FRAME

The Mother's words are all spoken in the twenty minutes that precede her death. The Old Man speaks at two
different moments, during the night where the Mother's
body is left lying on the floor, and at the time of the
Son's arrival. The Son's words are spoken on the third
day. The Mother's body is no longer in the house—the
Son will be attending her funeral the following day.

Their words overlap in certain scenes, although they are
not spoken at the same point in time.

Scene 1

FLASHING ON AND OFF

The Old Man enters The Mother's flat. The Son enters behind him. Both are carrying suitcases. The Mother is lying on the floor.

THE OLD MAN
(speaking to The Son)
I can't tell you much.
It happened.
Some kids.
They came to steal.
Steal what, don't ask me.

My eyes opened with the racket.
I came down in my pyjamas.
She was there. Right there. Stiff. Dead.

I looked around me.
Maybe...
I wanted to see her soul.
See it fly in the air free.
I didn't see a thing.
I stood there, for a long time.
It can take a while for the soul
to leave the body.

I didn't see a thing.
Just pictures behind my eyes.
Pictures of our life together.
Flashing on and off.

Silence.

Scene 2

ARRIVAL

THE SON
> I walk into the smell of the house from when I was
> as high as a small tree with red apples.

Scene 3

THE PICTURE

THE SON

I'm thinking about my mother. I mean, that woman I see in the picture. I'm five. The picture says I'm sitting on the crackly grey steps of the little porch outside our front door. I've got a Coca-Cola squeezed between my thighs. I was hot, the cold bottle feels good.

It's the Old Man upstairs who gave us the brown pop, to me and his son Simon who's ten. Behind the Kodak, it was the father of both of us, I know that now, who could see: me, my mother, and his son Simon.

We were looking at him with our squinched eyes. My mother, her mouth stretched, was smiling at the cake with no candles that she was holding with both hands to show her birthday to the Kodak.

A long face: the son Simon, I mean the old man's son, was sulking because I'm the one who was holding the bottle for the picture.

Then click. For one second, we were caught in the Kodak, the three of us, playing Teddy Tag, staying still like in a grave. A sharp memory.

Scene 4

STARTLED

THE MOTHER stands up. Under her, dried blood three days old. Aside from this stain, her clothes are clean. She spits on the bloodstain, then turns towards THE SON.

THE MOTHER
Pierre
you're here for real.
You gave me such a scare.
So much.
I almost hurt you again.
My God!

You came back to see me.
Come, let me hold you. *(He doesn't move.)*
I really wish you were here, for real.

Hungry? Thirsty? Anything?
A candy!

Hallowe'en tomorrow!
Last year I didn't have any candy.
When they came to the door
they had Hallowe'en faces.
It scared me through my mouth
they ran off.
One of them said really loud:
"She's a real witch."

   She laughs.

Got candy in my hand.
Your favourite.

My God
you've grown.

Look, rouge.
And lipstick.
Music.
Have to play some music.
It relieves the silence.

Do you think...
How do you think I look?
Any different? Disappointed in me, eh?
I look like a statue.
A statue of nothing.
I try to dress up more.
A skirt. High heels.
I fix my hair.

I wasn't expecting you anymore.
Ever.

Don't go looking through the medicine chest.
Those aren't candies, it's antrophene.
Otherwise my blood will coagulate.
I could get paralysed.
Last spring, I woke up paralysed on one side.
When I saw my fingers all crooked
my mouth shouted:
"Please, jesuses, please, not that,"
I prayed for two hours.
Crying.
I'd rather have them take me away.

She laughs.

Don't go looking in there again.
I'll close the door on your fingers.

Yes, it's come back.
The doctor told me:
"When your blood coagulates
a kind of epilepsy.
The brain jams."

Then I fall on the ground.
The body digs itself a hole in the floor.
A kind of magic I have.
A witch, ha! You bet.
Those pills prevent hole-digging.

I thought you'd never come back here again.
I called you so often.
I did.

I tried every one in the phone book.
All the Pierres, the Pierre Bellemares
Really, I'm sure.

If only you'd given me a hint
so I could find you.

Everywhere I called: no Pierre.
At the corner grocery store one day
I heard a man say:
"Pierre's a shoe salesman."
Pierre's come back at last, I said to myself.
Aren't you sick of playing with my shoes?
You pretended you were me, you wanted to make
me laugh.
You even talked like me.

I can feel the excitement, inside.
So happy.

The jesuses heard me:
"He has to come back to see me, my Pierre
just for a quick visit, to talk to me a bit.
At least a little bit.
I'd be the happiest woman ever."

Scene 5

A POTATO FIELD

THE MOTHER has gone back to lie on the floor. THE OLD MAN goes over to her, looks at her.

THE OLD MAN
    I wish I could cry.
    It won't come out.
    If I try, screw up my face
    I'll shout.
    Shouting breaks a man's backbone.
    Snap.
    Have to stand up straight as a fence post.
    A post in a fence around a potato field.
    Rotten. A field of rotten potatoes.
    Rotten.
    Poor little woman, your potato head is bleeding.
    Rotten. You're leaving your eyes, I can see that.
    Ice is taking over your body.
    I can't pick you up.
    A man's got to stand up straight when someone's fall-
    en down.

    If I stoop over to gather you up, I'll cry.
    I'm not a cloud over a potato field
    I'm just a post stuck
    in a field of rotten potatoes.

Scene 6

EXCITEMENT

THE MOTHER
(she stands up, excited)
Excitement catches a body off-guard.

I mean
it's my house here.
Sure. You lived in the house.
With me. But that's all.

You should've come back sooner.
I've been living alone, for ages.
Don't need anybody to live.

Just, just the jesuses.
All alone too much.
Good thing the jesuses get inside my body.
It's a relief. Otherwise I'll die.

Not even a quick phone call.
"Don't worry about me, I'm doing fine."
Some little sign of life at least.

Are you ashamed of me?
You never invited me to your store.
Maybe there were some shoes that fit me.

Heartless.

No news from you, nothing.
All alone, forever.
You wanted to make me cry
empty all the tears in my body.
Die drowned in my tears.

Lies.
Nothing but lies.
Even now, I know you're not here.
Just visions
inside the head of an almost dead woman.
Lies.

My eyes never cried over you.
You like the rest of them
wanting to punish me cause you left.
What did you want.
You want me to give you the clothes off my back?
That's what you want, here. Here.

She tears out her hair.

You want my whole life. Here, take it.

She spits on the floor.

Leave with all of me.
All of me, all of me.
Take it, all of it.
"Yes, jesuses, yes, I'm an ugly woman.
I gave birth to a dirty dog.
My little Pierre's a dirty dog."

She laughs.

I'll calm down.
Pierre, my little boy.
Why did you leave me all alone?

One day, I thought that Pierre would come back.
That Pierre would say:
"Forget all that, Mama. All is forgiven."
We could've gone off to hide in a life somewhere else.
Not let anyone know.

A bottle, two glasses.
To welcome you home.
Just once in a while.
Feels good.
Helps you disappear.

She empties the first glass in one gulp.

A real shock to see my Pierre again.
Drink up. (*THE SON doesn't move.*)
I'll drink this one thinking of you.

Your body changes.
Life makes sure of that, makes sure the body gets old.
Always caught off-guard.

Come here, so I can touch you. (*He doesn't move.*)

Scene 7

TEDDY TAG

The Son goes to find his mother's shoes and plays with them.

THE SON

One day, when I was little, I explained the teddy tag game to my mother. Let's say I'm the one who's holding the teddy, then you have to run so I don't catch you, if I touch you with the teddy, you freeze, frozen like a Kodak picture. You can't shout or talk. The other friends can unfreeze you, they have to come and set you free from the freezing. That's why, if it's me who has the teddy, I have to act scary like a polar bear, and run with eyes in the back of my head to catch everyone so they can't unfreeze you. Everyone's running all over the place, shouting, trying to scare each other. That's the game: afraid of being frozen by a bear. We always play teddy tag.

After that, she used to say I was a teddybear, she didn't say it often but I remember, Teddybear. I was her stuffed teddy. But I didn't want to be a stuffed teddy, that can't move, can't laugh, and just sits in the corner of a bedroom without saying a thing.

Scene 8

THE PHONE

THE OLD MAN
    I hate pressing the phone to my ear.
    It's for me.
    I have to take it.
    Besides, it's the bishop.
    A bishop friend.
    He gave me work when times were tough
    back when he was a priest.
    I was young.

    A bishop friend on the phone.
    For a favour.

    "Is the flat downstairs free?"
    "No, why?"
    "For a favour.
    I have to find a safe place for my sister to live.
    I need to see you."

    He came.
    "It's for my sister.
    Someone has to keep an eye on her.
    I'll pay you a bit more per month.
    I'll cover the cost of the flat.
    You just have to keep an eye
    on her from time to time.
    If she doesn't behave herself
    you can call me at this number.
    She'll be here in three days."

    Fine.

I couldn't refuse.
For a favour.
Three days to get the people downstairs out
that's a dirty landlord trick.
But for a favour.

Scene 9

THE LOVER UPSTAIRS

THE MOTHER
(as she takes out a picture that was well-hidden)
After the mess, the bishop told me to hide
the pictures so I wouldn't think about him.

I was twenty-seven
when I got away from the sisters.

> *She laughs.*

I had that. That little brat.
My little boy Pierre.

The daddy you never knew about, your daddy
you hear me, is the one who's taking the picture.
The old man upstairs.

The bottles of cold pop that he brought down
you'd drink them and laugh
sometimes with his son Simon too.

You can't keep things inside
otherwise you die with them.
You suffocate.
I say that…because it's coming out.
It has to come out while I'm dying.
To make peace with things in life.
I mean, things, you know?

The summer I was seventeen.
I had picked a pail of blueberries.

All by myself.
One of the neighbours from down the road
came up to the fence.
I was eating a handful of blueberries.
The neighbour was eating me with his eyes.
Without saying a word.

His hands took me.
"I want you to eat me up."
In my mind, I kept repeating it.
We ate all the berries together.

Two days before
I'd asked my mother
"Is it nice
being with a man?"
For an answer, my hungry body
got a taste of a wooden spoon.

"You do it to have children.
People forget the meaning of what must be
accomplished:
bearing children"
said my older brother, an educated priest.
I wasn't doing anything with my life.
"Won't make a nun or a wife," said my father.
He said that because of the neighbour down the
road
and another guy that same summer.
One of my brothers told on me.

   She spits on the floor.

They held a family meeting
and delivered the sentence:
leave my father's house.
"She has these spells, like she's possessed.
You take care of her, I can't stand the sight of her."
That's what my mother shouted at my educated
brother.
With both of the guys who got inside my dress
I asked them:
"Marry me.
We'll love each other till we die."
They laughed.
"You'll never be pure. A witch."
To prove it: I had a field
of little wild strawberries on my face.
Back at the house, I had fits
like epilepsy.
My mother was scared.
"Tell mama what's the matter."
She found out everything from my tattletale brother.

She spits again.

I left my father's house
to go to a mother house.
It was my brother, the educated priest
who placed me in the convent to work for the sis-
ters.
Sisters with a padlock under their black dresses.
They dressed me up like a housekeeper to clean
the dirt and the dustballs. (*little laugh*)
I kept thinking about the furballs between their legs.
In the fall, after the guys that summer
All the strawberries on my face went away.
The mother "inferior" (*little laugh*) said

I was becoming pure again.
But I thought it was
because of the broken padlock
under my white dress.

She laughs and spits on the floor.

I paid for two afternoons of pleasure
with ten years of darkness.
They always had to hide the witch of pleasure.
I still have fits, of epilepsy.
To escape from myself.
Break out of my bones. Out of the convent.

One day, I couldn't stand it anymore.
My body was twitching in my bed
in the mother house.
I wanted a man.
Like a pail full of blueberries.
A mouthful of fruit.

I told the bishop:
"I have to get out of the convent.
I can't go on like this
being a housekeeper here.
My body in a nun's cell.
I'm suffocating.
My body wants to have a baby
to be a mother."

I was thinking, while I was talking to him:
I want a man.
I want to be a mother lover.

She laughs.

My brother was holding my hands.
"I'll take care of that for my little sister."
Three days later, the bishop
true as the moon, helps me get out of there.
I'm twenty-seven when I get out.

My father brother says:
"I know somewhere you can live."
This flat, that's what he meant.
Because the old man upstairs
was a friend of the bishop's.

The old man upstairs was old
much older than me, I mean.
His family was already grown up.
Complete.
I didn't have to pay for the flat.
The old man upstairs helped me out.

One day, after I'd moved in
I thought to myself
he's a man
the old man upstairs.

I took him, here in this flat
like a wild woman, in sweat.
My skin shouted with joy, back then.
"Like a real witch"
that's what the old man upstairs used to say.

My body shouted and screamed inside
when he took his time
pushing down hard on me.
He wasn't bad for the age of his thing.
But sometimes, he was old.
He'd take a break.
I wouldn't say a word.
He'd smoke a couple of cigarettes.
He'd stare into space, breathing heavy through his
nose.

Then stomp out mad, shouting:
"All your fault, you're a witch."
He'd come back later.
He'd get on top of me again
but sometimes he was too old.
A big slap across my face.

Tears.

She laughs.

Sometimes she cries too.
I mean his wife.
The woman upstairs was sick.

Later, I realized that men are strict.
Too strict.
And mean.
Like the jesuses, they hit to punish you.

I got the child too.
I was filled with joy.
My own child.
I was twenty-eight.
I hid inside

my body of a twenty-eight-year-old mother.

My life stopped there.
I was twenty-eight.
For the first time in my life
I'd created something.
With the pleasure of my body.
It never happened to me again
being able to create.

She spits.

Never before. Never again.

Scene 10

FISH EYES

THE OLD MAN
> I want to tell you a secret.
> In your ear.
>
> In the floor upstairs
> I drilled fish eyes.
> I did it right away, a couple of weeks
> after you arrived.
> There…there…there. (*he points to the places*)
> To see into the witch's flat.
> Even into the bathroom.
> From upstairs, I could keep an eye on everything.
> Where you went, where you slept, where you
> cooked.
> Where you did everything.
> My eye riveted on you.
> A pretty little woman.
>
> The bishop came with you.
> Carrying suitcases.
> I only had eyes for you.
> I didn't let it show.
> Like I hadn't seen a thing. All I could see was you.
> When the bishop talks to me about you
> it's my chance to take a look.
> Perfectly natural. Question of appetite.
> A pretty little woman.
>
> The idea for the fish eyes…
> the idea flashed by like a train.
> In my head.

I took it seriously.
I have to keep an eye on the bishop's sister.
To see the pretty witch's body
without all the trappings of clothes.
One Sunday, the bishop came to get you.
A fall drive through the woods.
In the floor of the ceiling
I drilled secret eyes.

My wife stayed locked up in her bedroom.
A little pill in her tea
so she could have a deep sleep.
Covering up the holes was easy.
Under the rug, under the floor lamp, under the
linoleum.

When she woke up, my wife said:
"What's that?"
She doesn't talk. Mute.
With her eyes she asked: "What's that?"

My fingers clenched like a sledgehammer
in my hand, like a threat
yelling
so she could read every letter on my lips:
"What's that? Nothing, goddammit! Get out of the
way."
No more questions about the fish eyes
riveted in the floor.

The little blockhead
you know who I mean
Simon the youngest in the family
nosey-sneaky-creepy
with his twisted head
was rolling his eyes in the holes in the floor.

Bang! In his asshole.

He never tried again either.
Or asked any more questions.
A lesson for the whole family.
Those things are for me.
Mine. Period.

Simon
as he got older, he seemed less empty.
Because of his wife, she filled him up a bit.
One day he left, without warning.
Never came back.
We never saw him again.
That was at least ten, twelve years ago.
Took off to sow his oats, see the world.
I already told you that.
I'm repeating myself. An old man.

You never knew about the fish eyes,
did you?
That was just in the beginning.
Afterwards, I never looked anymore.
Just once in a while.

At first
especially when you went into the bathroom
I was there, upstairs, right away.
On my knees, my eyes glued to see you.
I played with myself between my legs.
My body flat on the floor.
In the tub or on the toilet
my fish eye saw you perfectly.
I kept an eye on you and I watched you too.
Stretched out full length, I let run down my pants
what it takes

especially if a man's on top of a woman.
The floor was hard and cold.
Cold. Bodies don't like the cold.
Heat makes you feel safe inside.
The cold makes a body nervous.

My arm isn't an auger
otherwise I would have pierced the floor
like a frozen lake in winter.
With the hand at the end of my arm
I could have touched your warm breasts
with their hard tips.
My arm isn't an auger.

Take the pretty young witch
in her bathroom.
My body was scorched from lying
on the icy linoleum.
I wanted her on top of my body
without the floor between us.
Warm skin.

One day, I went down the stairs
with my tool box.
"I've come to do some repairs."
To repair unbroken things.
I stayed a long time.
Lots of broken things.
I'd been watching her.
She didn't know it.
My fish eyes saw her naked, from head to toe.
My mother always told me:
"You're a clever toad!"

Scene 11

MY FIVE-YEAR-OLD BODY

THE SON

I was trying really hard. I was tugging on the arm of
the old man upstairs who'd come to take care of me
with his son Simon. Sometimes my mother went to
work as mother-of-housekeeping at the hospital.
The old man upstairs, I mean, the father of both of
us, had let his body go soft at one end of the sofa. I
was pulling really hard to wake him up, he'd drunk
too many of those brown bottles for adults. I didn't
realize that yet, I thought he was teasing me. Not
just me, but his son Simon too, cause he was pulling
on the other arm from the one I was pulling.

We pulled until he fell on the floor without meaning
to, just because we pulled too hard. Once he was on
the floor, he didn't budge an inch. He was drunk to
death inside, limp enough to die. With both our
strengths, we turned him over on his back. We were
laughing, me and the son Simon, and jumping up
and down on his belly and his heart.

We laughed until the night got dark, even our
stomachs were growling with hunger. His son
Simon, because of his empty head, started to cry.
Even after ten years of life, he didn't have a head
strong enough to be a big brother. I was smaller
than him, but I consoled him in my arms, he was
too heavy. He could have gone to get his deaf mother, but his head rang empty. Finally, I was the one
who went to get mine. When my snowsuit was on

my body, Simon's face cracked like the porch in tears, and through his big black teeth he said: "I'm scared to be alone in the flat."

My leg closed the door. Both my legs headed towards the hospital. My mother worked almost not often doing housekeeping, a job the old man upstairs found for my mother.

Cross the big road full of lights that kept moving. And the son Simon who I could still hear in the ears inside me: the sound of fear.

The dark outside made me hurry. I ran through the winter that had covered everything with snow. My body entered the hospital.

I yell, I yell: "Mama, Mama."

I stop in front of a door. A lady looks at me, with her coat on her back, a sick child in her arms for the emergency ward, and behind her a baby crying in the echo of the corridors.

A woman dressed in white comes over to me with something in her hands, asking me my name: Pierre Bellemare, and I want to talk to my mother-of-housekeeping because the old man upstairs had too much to drink because he'd rather live in my house. I think she doesn't believe anything I say. I tell her about the fear, the dark, the hunger, the empty-headed son Simon, the father of both of us on the floor like dead, and all of a sudden she goes to talk into a microphone, holding my hand.

"Pierre Bellemare's mother, Pierre Bellemare's mother." I wait in the corridor that's very long. Until

I see my mother's body changing from small to big because she was heading towards me. She was bouncing because of her legs that were walking very fast.

Then my five-year-old body stops moving. I say to myself: "Be a big boy, don't cry when you're in her arms," even though my body was crying inside on its own.

She came to fix everything in the flat, telling the old man that he lives upstairs even though she'd rather have him downstairs too. I think that after that, she didn't go back to work very often at the hospital as mother-of-housekeeping.

Scene 12

THE JESUSES' CLOTHES

THE MOTHER
You think I wasted my life.
You're wrong, kid.
I didn't always stay locked up
inside my unhappiness.

She spits and laughs.

Sometimes. I'd forget everything.
No memory that the son Pierre
the jesuses or even the old man upstairs
had ever been in my life.

Yeah, sometimes: I'd forget.

Went out a lot.
Sometimes to bingo, to get out of the house.
See other faces.
Paler than mine.
It's reassuring.
I'd study all the women
while they were placing their chips.
I never played, myself. Not so dumb.
I'd laugh inside.
A bunch of frustrated women playing.
Trying to get richer than their husbands.
So they could leave them behind.

Independent.
I was independent.
No husband, so to speak.

Plus my bit as a volunteer
it was the bishop who said to me:
"It will redeem you in the eyes of the
neighbourhood."
Saint Vincent de Paul Society
in the church basement.
During our break we could
eat cookies with a cup of tea or coffee.
Suit yourself.
"Three brown cookies with cream filling
and a coffee, milk-and-sugar, please."

We sorted out the donated clothes.
A mountain of clothes.
Every spring and every fall.
Hard to believe people wore all that.
Really incredible.

I got my clothes there.
Except for my underwear.

Just for fun
I put costumes
for a whole family
on hangers.
A daddy, a mummy and some kids
from head to toe.

A hat, a tuque, a cap
shirt, tie
blouse, skirt
pants, belt, suspenders
socks, shoes
mittens, coat
depending on the season, of course.

Not so dumb.

Once, I chose a crazy mix.
Made specially for the women who play bingo.
A hockey helmet
a sexy mini-skirt
a tie
woolen mittens
no sweater but a bra
with shoes that didn't match.

I could see them all sitting there, transformed.
Bingo monsters out of moth balls.
The boss (*she spits on the floor*)
the lady in charge of the clothes counter
she didn't think it was funny.

Anyway, I knew what I meant.

When no one was looking
behind a row of clothes
I'd dress up all sorts of people.
I did it just so I could laugh inside.

I couldn't see them
but I knew they were there.
Just so I could laugh at them.

I never showed them to anyone.
My arrangements.
The boss, the same one as before
(she spits again)
suspected me for a long time.
Because one day
somebody disguised
in the craziest get-ups

all the holy statues
in the church.

That was the time I almost
died laughing inside.

Scene 13

BLOODSUCKER LAKE

THE OLD MAN
> The skin on your body is warm.
> The sun gets inside.
> Your body needs to go for a swim.
> In the water.
> In the water of Bloodsucker Lake.
> "I'm going out," I mouth the words for the wife,
> "I'm taking the kid with me.
> And the kid downstairs too.
> Me, Simon, Pierre and his mother."

> We leave in the car
> with the wind pushing my Chevrolet.
> Blowing hair everywhere.
> "Stop whining, blockhead.
> If Pierre's in the front, he's in the front."

> Pierre's mother presses against my leg.
> I drive straight ahead, eyes on the road.
> The engine sounds good.
> A song starts running through my head.
> My radio doesn't work.
> A song made up in my head.
> The words change.
> Depending upon how I feel.
> Right now, I'm happy.
> Pierre's mother's making me feel
> like the wind in a field.
> A field of potatoes.
> I always see the same field of potatoes.

It keeps coming back.

When I was young, really little
me and my father, we used to go dig
the potatoes in the field.
I can see my father's smile.
He'd just thrown a potato at my bum.
I was bent over.
I jumped up and yelled.
My father was laughing. He kept on smiling.
So happy in the wind in the field.

Ten minutes later
the old man fell
face down in the field of potatoes.
His heart fell into the earth.
Just broke down.
I kept throwing potatoes at him.
I wanted to hear him laugh
but I was all alone, crying.
His heart had gone into the earth.

Whenever I'm happy, I think
of the field and the wind.
Whenever I'm sad, I think
of the potatoes.

My song is about Pierre's mother's hair.
A smile on my lips.
I'm also thinking about dirty things.
Her breast in my mouth.
My tongue groping.
She pulls down my pants.
Her tongue in my ear.
Dirty words: cunt-cock
Cunt-cock, cunt-cock.

"Take my vagina."
I can hear her saying it to me.

I'm still driving.

She puts her hands in the wrong place and says:
"Do you feel like it?"
The words burst out of my eyes.
Cunt-cock.

THE MOTHER
(whispering)
I didn't know what to do with myself
I didn't know what to do with my arms
or my legs or anything else.

Except with the old man upstairs.
My body became totally different.
The rest of the time, emptiness.
That's why I gave up
the cleaning job at the hospital.
That way he could come
whenever he wanted.
He didn't come often.

One of God's whores maybe.

Burst of laughter.

THE OLD MAN
I can hardly wait.
On the black and red plaid blanket.
The skin of our two bodies together.
That's what it's for, Bloodsucker Lake
pressing up against each other.
With nobody else on the little beach.

Once the kids are in the water
we hide in the woods.
First, we tell Pierre:
"Look at the watch:
don't come for us until the hands
are like this."
Now we don't have to worry.

Bloodsucker Lake.

The pretty young witch.
Happiness doesn't exist.
I've told you that before.
But the time when the wind was most beautiful
in my whole life, I'm telling you
the most beautiful wind in my life was you.
The wind.

Bloodsucker Lake.
Stealing your blood.
"Don't stand still in the mud
or they'll get your blood!"

That afternoon
no snuggling on the red and black blanket.
The four of us were there our feet in the bloodsuck-
er water
watching an airplane land.
Like a duck.
The propellers turn with the noise.
Pierre was shouting: "An airplane, a real airplane."
On the beach was a little dock.
The plane turned off its engines at the little dock.
Nothing else in sight, just us and the plane.

We went over holding hands.
The pilot is adding some oil.
He talked to me about the clear sky
I talked about the summer sun with a cigarette.

"Come for a ride.
Bring someone
there's room for two."

How to choose who?
The sun was burning my eyes.
"Come, Pierre, we're going up in the sky.
Shh, blockhead, stop whining for nothing!
If I decide: Pierre, we're going up in the sky
we're going up in the sky.
That's it. Period."

Sitting in the plane, we were vibrating.
We were saying goodbye with our hands.
To Simon and you.
The more we waved
the higher we went.
Like ducks with their wings
Pierre was grabbing onto my pants.
He was shrieking with excitement.
Even louder than the engine.
I can still hear him.
"It's so small, a small mother, a small Simon
so small
small-small like toy dolls."
Pierre's heart was bouncing with laughter in his
throat.

Joy, it's something you don't hear often.
A child is so beautiful in the sky
especially when his heart laughs by itself.
Over the lake, in the sky
I looked at Pierre. I saw my Pierre.
A beautiful little Pierre made of my skin.

Sundays, when it was hot
we'd go for a ride in the car
all the way to Bloodsucker Lake.
When you come back, Pierre, we'll talk.
Together we'll remember
some happy times.

Scene 14

FLATS FOR FEET

THE SON

During the daytime, a shoe, a shoe, a shoe, a shoe. When it got into my hands and feet, I'd gallop across the floor to say I was playing horse. My teeth ate the rungs of chairs when I was hungry for hay; I'd drink some water from the bowl I put under the table before the game. With a burst of strength that shook the ground, the horse jumped out of its shoes and flew into the sky. The shoes go looking everywhere, in the closets, in the oven, on the walls, out the windows. No more horse.

During the sleeptime, the red shoes and the blue ones with the white bows were tucked in under my bed, and I was sleeping too. The horse got back into the shoes when morning and sunshine climbed onto my bed.

During the daytime, we play at galloping across the floor again. Sometimes, I let my ear lie on the floorboards so I could hear my mother's steps.

When they go outside, people put on shoes so they don't fly into the sky. Shoes keep you on the ground. My feet who live in a little house so they can see the world.

Scene 15

THE HOTEL ROOM

THE MOTHER
Everything I'm going to tell you now
it all happened before the mess.
Before you left.

In the late spring
the yellow of morning was running through the
trees
with the green leaves, the branches of birds.

And you were playing outside.
Always.
What were you playing?

On the stereo.
I was playing a song
that the old man upstairs had given me.
My mouth was singing.
The water was filling the tub.
I was undressing my body.

My body was singing.
That song that fills the head
with love.

My mouth was giving kisses to my arm.
My tongue couldn't keep still.

In the mirror
the eyes were looking at my undressed body.
After, I'd get into the hot bath.
My head was full of those men

I used to see in the store catalogues.

With the heat of the water, and the yellow of
morning
slipping into my bath
my wild eyes would choose
a man from the catalogue.

We meet in a hotel.
The man from the catalogue comes up close
he whispers in my ear:
"Hello there."

I'm not surprised.
My story happens slowly
so I can make it last.
I felt like it was almost real.
My belly said it was, too.
The man, you know, with the new suit.
Broad shoulders.
We're at the Adam and Eve Hotel.

I went there once, to that hotel.
Before going to the convent
just to wait
to get warm.
My mother gave me a spanking.
I was a "slut" to go there.

I'm in the Adam and Eve Hotel
with the man that I chose for love all over.
There's lots of laughing.
Lots of drinking.
And dancing.
Looking at each other.
Like in the movies.

Just the two of us. In the eyes.
The looks make the breathing faster
with a wanting in the man's eye.
A little nod of the head and a smile.
And I'm headed upstairs with him.

That's when I close my eyes.

My heart's banging hard
a bell in my body
cause love was vibrating everywhere.
With the soap, I gave myself shivers
that grabbed that belly of mine.

Through the window of the hotel room
the air outside smells of spring.

Hands and mouth race all over the body.
The breathing is talking loud.
Our hurry laid us on the bed almost dressed.
Our throats are laughing, our bellies twitching.

All of a sudden the old man upstairs comes into the
house.
I get out of the tub.
My story is still going on.
My eyes are half-closed, in a kind of dream.
I force my head to think that the old man upstairs
is the chosen man.

I head for the bed, as soon as he takes my body
it cries out for more while my head is thinking
of the man in the hotel room.

The old man upstairs didn't know
that in my head I saw something else.
Every time I went
to that hotel in my head with some men
and the old man upstairs appeared just then
he'd say I was too much of a squirmer
too much of a witch
and he couldn't concentrate.

Because of my voice, you know.
The sounds that came out of my mouth.
Screams that came from my belly.
I didn't even recognize myself.
I became a woman in a catalogue.
His hand would cover my mouth.
To prevent. Everything. Everything.
The sound of my voice could reach
the sky when I was at the Adam and Eve Hotel.

After the mess
the old man upstairs was never the same either.

Once, it happened again.
The hotel, I mean.
The old man upstairs is strict
he's the one who pays for my flat.
The fist hit me in the face.
It almost made me cry.

Never.
I'm telling you after that
I never went back to the men from the catalogue.
I never thought about the Adam and Eve Hotel
again.

She spits.

Scene 16

THE UNBURIED KODAK

THE SON

Shirley the daughter, my half-sister, the daughter of the old man upstairs came back with a beautiful yellow wedding car to tell us about her honeymoon. My mouth, like a bee on a flower, would have liked to kiss her coloured cheek that always smelled of perfume. Shirley the daughter moved out from upstairs a long time ago. Whenever she came, it was always a wedding party, I wanted to marry her so much.

Me and the son Simon, the blockhead, not saying a thing. We were sitting with the shadow of the sun, against the garage doors in the gravel driveway, when she walked by with her husband.

Through the car window, on the black seat, my curious hand saw her Kodak. I didn't know that a Kodak was a Kodak. I just saw a toy that was a toy, with lots of buttons.

My curious hand started again. I went to hide in the weeds behind the garage. Lots of long-legged spiders got scared when they saw us. The son Simon hid me from the sun.

The Kodak from the daughter Shirley's love trip!

When I opened it, there was a yellow spool with red writing. A piece of ribbon was sticking out of the spool. I pulled on it: a long ribbon!

It looked like the ones Mama hung in the house; the flies got stuck, and you could tell they were dead after a while. The flies didn't move anymore, they stayed frozen like statues. There was some product on the ribbon that attracted them and pfft! the legs or the wings got stuck on it. When my mother threw out the ribbon full of black flies, the garbage pail ate them during the night.

I threw the black ribbon of pictures into the weeds to see if the spider flies would get stuck on it. Nothing worked. Not even in the weeds. A useless decoration.

The next day, after I'd hidden it in a treasure hole, I asked the old man upstairs what Kodaks were for, because at night, on the porch steps, back and forth, from my mother to the old man, from the old man to my mother, they were talking about his daughter Shirley's Kodak: disappeared into thin air.

Then I realized that beside the Kodak, I'd buried a ribbon with lots of memories stuck to it. But I hadn't seen anything, probably because they weren't my memories.

The son Simon got one hell of a kick that nobody saw: he just felt like saying with his ribbon of a tongue full of flies that there was a treasure hole with a Kodak in it. The blockhead was crying inside, the kick hurt him, right here on the shin where it burns. He finished his pop before me, not daring to say a thing.

Before falling asleep, under my bed in the flat, I looked at all the drawings I'd created with my fingers during the year at kindergarten. I couldn't see them very well because of the dark, but I imagined that I'd taken some beautiful pictures, memories from my life.

The next morning, when my legs got me out of bed even earlier than my mother, I saw the son Simon with his mouth making all kinds of faces that got me outside in a flash.

I see the unburied Kodak dangling on his stomach, hanging around his neck. I think of the kick I gave him and I say: "Leave that alone or I'll make a hole in your blockhead."

Then he shouted, just for my ears: "You dirty dog, you're a bastard, a dirty dog bastard." He pulls down his pants and shows me his white summer bum, and then he lets out a fart, just for my ears.

I looked at him without saying or doing a thing. Only my teeth in my mouth were cracking. It tasted like metal in my throat. I could feel a wave of black heat creeping up my neck. His bum and his stupid faces woke up a dog in my belly. Tight as a knot, with a dog racing through my body like smoke.

I burst out of myself in a fit, shouting: "A dirty dog bites." His legs took off, with me racing after him. He dropped the Kodak so he could run faster. My curious hand picked it up off the gravel. "I'm going to hit you over the head with a picture." Him and his fear went to hide, with all the doors locked, in Shirley's love car. It was a fast, crazy race.

In the back seat, the son Simon, with his toad face, is making more faces at me, he even glues his flabby bum to the car window. My feet were biting at the dust.

One more toad face: I threw my arm behind me, and the Kodak went flying through the air. The crash was sharp and surprising. I'd just hit him right in the face. A broken window and an expensive Kodak.

The old man upstairs was surprising too, with the roar of a beast when he rushed downstairs. He picked up a piece of wood lying on the gravel. You could see rage all around him. That rage pulled down my pants and yanked up my arm, really high like a side of beef on a butcher's hook, and my bare bum received the blows.

During the beating, the son Simon was smiling at me, all sneaky joy through the car window. As I pulled up my pants, my eyes filled with sweat, slaps were drilling holes in the back of the blockhead's head. Yelping like a stuck pig, he ran upstairs to his house, holding his head. The old man upstairs gave my mother dirty looks as he climbed the stairs with the broken Kodak in his hand.

And wham, our fierce games were over, drowned in a puddle of tears. Sometimes, me and the son Simon, we laughed, sometimes we cried. That's all.

Things were different with my mother. No laughs, no tears. After the beating on the meat hook, my mother watched me head into the house without saying or doing a thing. She'd seen it all from her bedroom window, along with everything else, I'm sure.

Lots of times she watches me from the window when I play to be seen. Every time I see her, I give her a smile, but her mouth never says anything. She looks at me like a dog walking by.

Once I said to Simon: "Look at my mother, she looks like a picture glued to the window."

Sometimes I thought: a dead mother.

Scene 17

THE BROKEN MOON

THE MOTHER, THE SON and THE OLD MAN are caught up in a circular movement that evokes a trance. THE SON is giggling.

THE OLD MAN
The mother is carrying a child
everything's round, inside and out.

THE MOTHER
Pierre, Pierre
Say something, Pierre.

THE OLD MAN
Pierre, a sunny child who's mine too.

THE SON
In my mouth I have a laugh that bounces to the roof
of my tongue and my hide-and-seek hand holds
back the laugh so that woman who's looking for me
can't find me.

THE OLD MAN
I did a lot of heavy drinking.
I drank but it didn't make things better.
I couldn't come live with the two of you.
Because of the other family upstairs.

THE MOTHER
     I know you're in your room.
     Come out of there.
     Stop fooling around.
     Stop laughing.
     If you don't…

THE OLD MAN
     Pierre was always playing tricks
     to get you to laugh.
     You never laughed.

THE SON
     When the moon was really round and I hadn't seen
     it yet, when I saw it all of a sudden, like it was say-
     ing "hello" to me by surprise, my legs turned to jello,
     all soft and shaky.

THE MOTHER
     A fit comes fast, Pierre.

THE OLD MAN
     With that mess, you took my son away from me.
     I loved him with all my heart.

THE MOTHER
     A shock in your head.
     Epilepsy.
     Bang, you're paralysed.

THE SON
     Some day, I used to say, I was going to touch the
     moon with my hand. A moon is no bigger than
     twenty-five cents.

THE MOTHER
     You hear me, kid!

THE SON

I could keep it in my pocket. When it got too dark in my room, I could take it out and light up my drawings or whatever I want.

THE OLD MAN

I'd like to shout but it breaks a man's backbone.

THE SON

With my fingers, standing on the tips of my ten toes, I took the moon. I've got it hidden on me right here.

THE MOTHER

Give it to me.
I know what you've got.
You stole from your mother.
You stole some money.

THE OLD MAN

He didn't steal a thing, he was playing.

THE SON

I could make the moon roll like a yo-yo.

THE MOTHER

Give it to me.

THE OLD MAN

I can't understand it. Can't get it through my head.

THE MOTHER

Give it to me.

THE SON

I hide here without telling. I'm going to lend the twenty-five cent moon to anyone who falls into black holes of fear.

THE MOTHER
>Come out from under the bed.
>Come out, Pierre.
>If you don't…
>Stop laughing.
>Wait.
>The fit is coming.

THE SON
>Nobody better find it in my room, or in my pockets,
>or anywhere. A moon thief! (*He laughs heartily*.)

THE MOTHER
>You're deaf.
>You're mute.
>You're dumb.
>A filthy little beast
>like a dirty dog.

THE OLD MAN
>She kept saying: "No husband in the house,
>no happiness in the house."
>Things started to go wrong with her sunny son.

THE MOTHER
>Stop fooling around.
>Shut up, shut up.
>Wait till I catch you.
>Come back here.

THE SON
>A moon thief. That's what my head said to me
>whenever I saw the moon.

THE MOTHER
 I'll tear up your drawings.
 All of your drawings.

THE OLD MAN
 A child isn't a teddybear, it's alive.
 That boy doesn't have a bad bone in his body.

THE SON
 My drawings that I love, it was my fingers who
 made those drawings.

THE MOTHER
 Let go of me.

THE SON
 My drawings. Don't touch them.

THE OLD MAN
 I wish I'd been there.
 But I wasn't. That's all there is to it.

THE MOTHER
 Stop it. Stop living.

THE OLD MAN
 I'm going to shout.

THE SON
 (repeating)
 My drawings from my fingers.

THE MOTHER
 I don't want anything to do with you.

THE OLD MAN
 I'm going to shout.

THE MOTHER
  Harder and harder.
  Something's bleeding under the blanket.

THE OLD MAN
  I'm going to shout.

THE MOTHER
  The fit is going to kill you.

THE OLD MAN
  I wanted to say it: "Stop, stop."
  I wasn't there, that's all there is to it.

THE MOTHER
  Get out of the way, Pierre.
  Run.
  My arm has epilepsy.

THE OLD MAN
  Some day I'm going to shout.

  THE SON falls silently.

THE MOTHER
  Look how it digs holes.
  Look how hard my arm can hit.
  Too hard, too hard.

  They stop going round in circles. Deep silence.

THE OLD MAN
  Some day, I'm going to shout.
  The moon will shatter.
  There's a pack of wolves in my throat.

Scene 18

RED FORGIVENESS

THE MOTHER won't speak to THE SON again, from now on her words will be directed to THE OLD MAN.

THE MOTHER
    The child Pierre wasn't making a noise.
    Just looking with his eyes that were crying
    without tears.
    Afraid maybe
    because of the scissors
    that were running over his body.

    He wasn't screaming.
    Just blood and the strength of the arm
    going up and down my Pierre's body.
    Inside I kept telling myself, through my eyes, to
    stop.
    I kept telling my arm, screaming.
    But my arm was deaf.

    I was having an epileptic fit
    in my arm.
    It wasn't me who wanted to hurt Pierre.
    My belly had made a beautiful baby
    and only my arm wanted to kill him.

    The red blood everywhere was making a mess of the
    bedroom.
    Silence at last, all around that child of mine.

    When the child Pierre
    came out of me all red
    surrounded by joy

when the hospital laid him between my breasts.

My Pierre was breathing in the silence.

It takes a long time
to make the bedroom in the flat
clean.

After that, I didn't notice my wrinkles
or my grey hair.
After that, silence never went away.

It takes a long time
a life long time for forgiveness.

She spits on the floor.

Scene 19

NO NAME FOR THE BODY

THE OLD MAN
My tongue is hot.
Like a potato.
I can't stop talking.
If my wife had died a long time ago
I would have brought you upstairs.
Kept you close to me.
To live, sleep, eat, everything.
I hate life. I've hated my life.
Life takes over.
We see it in a different way, life.
We think it's different, even while we're living it.
We're never there in life.

The head is here, let's say
the feet go in the opposite direction
the arms that way, and our red heart goes round
in circles.
Our heart aches.

I can feel a fever rising from my feet to my head.
Now I'm going to shout.

Goddam body, goddam skin.
You shrivel me up, you crush my bones
between the joints, you freeze me.
I'd like to have a body
a kind of body with no words
a body like a tree or the wind.
There shouldn't be a name for the body.
We could call it: the nothing.

It would be in life
like the wind in a field
a sun with other suns.
I'm red with anger.
Goddam sky.
My tongue is hot.

My backbone is breaking.
I'm in a field of potatoes
lying with my face against the sky.

If the stars
are fish eyes
I curse the people
with their dirty eyes watching us.

I want to feel
the peace of the summer sun.
The peace of the summer sun.

Scene 20

THE WHITE HOSPITAL, THE BLACK HOSPITAL

THE MOTHER
  I told the bishop
  when the old man upstairs called him:
  "A mess, just a mess.
  Because of my arm.
  I couldn't stop it."

  I felt sorriness deep into the bone of my arm.
  But no tears came out anywhere.
  I froze, froze all over.

  It's still ringing everywhere
  through the plaster walls of the prison
  the words spoken by the bishop to his friend
  the judge:
  "With your consent, I'll take care of her."
  After a silence, the judge says:
  "My lips are sealed."

  Late at night, hidden in the car
  the bishop didn't say a word to me
  his lips are sealed.
  Come morning
  he whispers to the mother superior:
  "We'll hide the unwed mother, in the convent."

  The bishop hid the mother-witch
  in a convent.

THE SON

One day my mother wasn't around me any more. Disappeared. I wanted to get up but it wouldn't work because of the hospital bed that was holding me there all white.

My nose was full of the smell of medicine spinning in my dizzy head. The sound of babies crying was whining in the inside of my ears, deep inside like a cut you want to rub away with your hands. Tear out the babies' cries, throw them in the washer-wringer so they don't whine anymore, so they smell soft and clean. My mother must have put me here so they could take care of me during her housekeeping work.

A lady with a tray came over to me, my eyes open a tiny slit, just enough to pretend I was sleeping and see everything at the same time. A nice "good morning" from a lady in your ear makes you want to see your mother. Even if I didn't know her, I let her see my back, my stomach, my legs, even my embarrassed bum. Her touching hurt in my hurt spots. Even with the slit of my eyes, I couldn't see anything. My face worked hard so it wouldn't hurt, but she kept tearing the red and white things off my skin. I couldn't understand why with her gentle voice, she was playing a hurting game. But I don't want to cry because I don't want to go into the washer-wringer. It's overflowing in my mouth: cries, calls for my mother, yells: Simon help. The gentle hurting lady was talking to me to make me brave.

A man with a heart-listener told me I was wounded with holes of dried blood and that inside me where I

couldn't see, muscles and other things were broken.
"While it's healing, it's going to hurt and afterwards,
you'll be healed" is what the heart-listening man
said. After that I wanted the gentle hurting lady to
hurt me so it would heal faster. Sometimes, even in
the middle of the night, I'd wake up in the white bed
whining with pain. It hurt, really hurt. I was whining all over, but under my lips was a smile of joy,
"I'm going to heal fast because of the bad hurt."

THE MOTHER

Thirty months. Thirty months.
One noon a sister hissed at me
nobody else heard her: "Witch"
with a little spit
that trickled down my arm.

The fit came back in a flash.
Fingernails can scratch a face.

She laughs.

Never ate with the black sisters again
not for prayers either.
I had to pray two hours longer.
But I wasn't saying anything inside my head.
Just pretending.
Sometimes I even fell asleep
right there on the kneeler.

After the mess
I never said another word from the sealed lips
in my sealed head.

Never laughed.
Or cried.

Just watched. That's all.
With the jesuses all around who were watching too.
After the mess with the child Pierre
it was the jesuses that kept ringing in my ears.
Forgiveness takes a long time coming.
It catches life off-guard, forgiveness does.

THE SON

By the end, I knew all the gentle ladies. I had at
least ten of them taking care of me. Not at the same
time! All kinds of ladies, a mix like the candies the
pretty gentle lady gave me when the other kids
weren't looking. The one who made me laugh the
most was the fat gentle lady. The one who was the
nicest patter was the perfumed gentle lady. Her
perfume made me forget the white and the medicine. Perfumed patting.

The old man upstairs came to see me with the son
Simon and a doggy in his hands to give me as a
present for a bedtime-friend. His old doggy smelled
of his stuffy house. When the perfumed gentle lady
came at night to put me to bed with the other
dreamy kids in the room, I asked her to hold the
doggy close to her, to hug it really, really hard. Even
with the perfume, the dirty brown foam doggy still
smelled bad.

When the hands of the perfumed gentle lady
touched my skin, because she went under my white
hospital dress pyjamas, she'd touch the places
where there were no holes. I didn't talk much. I listened to her hand talk about patting. Sometimes I'd
turn over so the rest of my body wouldn't feel sad
cause it wasn't touched.

It was an ugly boy who came to tell me that my murderer mother had tried to kill me. It was the fat gentle lady who told me what murder-crime-prison meant. I wanted to see my not killer mother, in my arms like always, to say: "Take me back, mama, I'll never be bad again, I'll never make you mad again, take me back, mama."

The perfumed gentle lady would say "be brave" while my nose raced around stocking up on her smell, so that when she wasn't there, I could just say "Come close to me, perfume lady." Like a magic word that could make me smell from inside me her perfume of patting. Every time, it always worked. As soon as the smell came back, I could feel her gentle hands touching me. And I'd tell myself it was my mother.

One morning the heart-listener man came to say goodbye to me, because of the healing that meant I had to leave. All the gentle ladies gave me goodbye kisses and smiles with a wooden train. Eight pieces: red, black, blue, yellow, with a bit of green all over, and letters in gold writing. A present train from the gentle ladies so I could leave with carfuls of good luck, cars full of luck in life. My hand was holding my wooden toy in a brown paper bag, and on my back an outfit the old man upstairs bought me for getting out of the hospital. Simon was holding my other hand.

THE MOTHER

In the convent, the bishop had hidden the mother-witch.

THE SON AND THE MOTHER
Three months later.

THE SON
I saw my mother again.

THE MOTHER
They called me to the parlour.
On the other side of the screen
a little boy was crying:

THE SON
"Mama, mama." I saw my mother one last time, all
dressed in black, even her face was black with
shadows. Her white teeth kept repeating:

THE MOTHER AND THE OLD MAN
"I can't keep you."
"Child-murderer mother."

THE MOTHER
Open the wound.
Bring him to see me one last time
so I could hold him
hug him a bit.
On my lap
he asked me:

THE SON AND THE OLD MAN
"Why the black dress?
Why can't we go home?"

THE SON

I wanted to pat her under her black hospital dress
pyjamas, and tell her: "During the healing, it will
hurt, and afterwards you'll be healed and we'll be
together."

THE MOTHER

His eyes were asking me things
and I kept answering:

ALL THREE

"I can't keep you
I can't keep you."

THE SON

I wanted to tell her lots of words with my tongue
but I was crying too hard because they were sepa-
rating us and I was wondering why everybody else
was crying too. Even Simon.

THE OLD MAN

(to THE MOTHER)
I'd like to give you
something from me
a little something
to make you feel good.
I took a little box of chocolate
out of my jacket pocket.
But I didn't say a thing.

THE SON

It's the first time I ever saw the old man upstairs
with salty water in his eyes running like tears when
he handed her a little sugary present.

THE MOTHER
>Behind the screen, my son was leaving
crying from his child's belly
until the iron door was locked.
Then I left, fainting on the floor.

THE MOTHER AND THE SON
>Opening the wound makes you pass out.
Fall into a hole where nobody can follow.

Scene 21

THE SON'S SOMEWHERE ELSE

THE OLD MAN
> I hate the phone.
> Putting my mouth so close
> it makes me think of kissing
> with the person at the other end of the line.

> For a favour.
> "Hello.
> Could you do your brother a favour.
> Take a beautiful, nice Pierre.
> The bishop will pay for his food and everything.
> You'll keep him at your place.
> Our secret.
> You'll never bring him back here.
> I'll be right there, with him."
> My brother wears his heart on both hands.
> He welcomes people with an open heart.

> His wife didn't like Pierre.
> I could see it right away.
> He didn't stay in school for long.
> My brother's wife
> sent Pierre to work in the shoe factory.

> Sometimes I went up to see him.
> It was a long drive.
> He'd ask me for news.
> I'd say:
> "Your mother's gone, we don't know where.
> And how are you doing?"

He still laughed a lot.
But not like when he was little.

I didn't know what to say.
What to say to replace
a mother's words.
My words were too short.
I never talked to my kids.

I could only say
my hand on his neck:
"Be brave!"

THE SON

It was a long, silent drive. Simon was sleeping, with his head heavy even if it was empty on my thigh, and with my wooden train beside me. We drove to a somewhere else that I didn't know. The car stopped in the dark.

"You're going to live here now," said the mouth of the old man who was my father. "I want to go back home." He made signs with his hands and his head to show me he still felt sorry on his cheeks, telling me with his lips that trembled: "We can't, it's the law." Far from home. People I didn't know.

I closed my teeth tight so I couldn't say a thing. Silent as a turtle. My father told me their names; they talked to me; I kept playing the deaf ear and the frozen tongue. I did everything wrong, even when I knew how to do it right. I skipped my home-work at school. On purpose, just to say how mad I was to be there in a house somewhere else that I didn't want. "Where's my mother?" I kept shouting at the mean, ugly woman who took care of me.

She'd answer by making a face at me, shouting in my ears some ugly word to say her hate "yukk." She couldn't stand the sight of me, and I never snuggled her.

My name was Pierre, but they said I was a rock; later on, they said I was a turtle. The kids in that family never knew who I was, they called me "turtle" because they said I was slow in my head and that I never came out of my shell. They didn't understand, my head made itself hard so I wouldn't have to be with them. Sometimes I wanted to make holes all over their bodies because I felt so much hate for the family that made fun of me. Except for the husband of the mean, ugly woman. He was nice to me, but not as nice as my father who I saw just once in a while.

I stayed inside my train, like I was made of wood, with the colours black, red, blue, yellow and a bit of green all over, with letters in gold writing. I never came out, I was waiting for my lucky chance.

Some day I'd leave to find my mother, in a train, a real one. I never forgot my mother, I just forgot to leave. I stayed in the place where the father upstairs put me.

THE MOTHER
After thirty months
the bishop took me out of the room in the convent
so I could go back to the flat.

The old man upstairs
was the bishop's friend.
He'd kept the flat

till I came back.

"She's gone on a trip, to see her family," he'd say.
The flat hadn't changed, not a bit.
Except for the blood from the mess.
Even after scrubbing.
The old man upstairs says:
"It's impossible to get rid of blood
it's a person's soul."

"Time heals all things," says the bishop.
"The child has been adopted," we were supposed to
say.

Far away.

"Now, as long as the prayers don't stop,
you'll never be alone again," says the bishop.
I understood:
the jesuses will be with you and inside you.
If nightmares come, the jesuses will be there.

The mess stayed for a long time in my flat.
It was my head that kept bringing it back.
When I got home, that's when I cried.

THE OLD MAN
When I went to see Pierre at my brother's
I always thanked him before I left.
"Isn't his mother ever going to take him back?
I can't keep him forever."

With his open heart, he kept him forever.
When he was twenty-one, we set him up on the
same street.
My brother's street. In a rooming house with board.
The bishop had said:

80

"Pierre is forbidden to see his mother again.
His mother is forbidden to see her Pierre again."

When I went into town
after the mess
curious tongues
asked me news about Pierre.
For an answer they got:
"None of your business."
Rumours told the story
backwards.

I opened my trap.
Can't let the filthy gossips
get away with their rumours.
I cleaned up the rumours
by telling the truth.
The whole town knew
about Pierre.
"Don't tell the mother.
And stop asking questions."

All those years, I saw Pierre grow.
A father can stop being a father, if he decides to.
A mother is always a mother.
It comes from the belly.

One day, I asked Pierre to tell me about his life.
I listened to him talk to me.
His life stopped with the mess.
After that, nothing.
Inside he kept his child's head.
Even at school.
He repeated lots of years.
Unhappiness makes you lose your intelligence.
Some day, the child Pierre will be reborn.

His intelligence will return.

THE SON

One day I'd grown up so much, it was time to move to another house, on my own, to be independent, said the father upstairs: "Some day you'll get married."

Afterwards, I started to work in a factory where shoes were getting made, I nailed on the heels. The noise always made lots of tapping, my eyes burned with the sharp smells of shoes. The shoe owner gave me a chance: selling shoes in the store in the front of the factory. It didn't last long because I didn't know how to say the right things, so instead I did the cleaning in the factory behind the store and in the selling store, and ran errands for the owner. It was better than making leather shoes, mostly because of the errands. I walked down the street, my chin in the wind. The owner sent me on missions. Everything was alive all around me, with the noise of the lights in the street, and the cars in the traffic.

On my missions as deliverer of repaired shoes, of new shoes for other stores, of closed envelopes, on my way I had to enter big stores that sold all kinds of things, clothes, umbrellas, toys, dresses with the colours of my train everywhere. And especially a place that sold perfume. All kinds of perfume with a pretty makeup lady. Her mouth spoke to me in red. "Can I help you?" Embarrassment grabbed my face and lowered it. I left without saying or doing anything. I didn't want to be a turtle with her because she smelled good.

With my saved up money, I went to buy myself some perfume from the pretty makeup lady. Flowers in a bottle that I push-pushed over my sleeping bed before I fell asleep. A touch of perfume.

In my head I said the magic formula: "Come close to me, perfume lady." She came, except now it was the pretty makeup lady who touched me. Once when I made up my mind, I went to give her a nice present all wrapped up in red and yellow ribbon, a chain with a medal shaped like a heart to put around her neck and on her big pointy breasts. On the heart-shaped medal, the jewelry man wrote on the gold of my savings: "more than yesterday, less than tomorrow." It took almost a long time for the jewelry man to explain the "more than yesterday, less than tomorrow." But finally, it really was a nice jewel of words from the heart. With a little smile, she gave me her hand to shake mine.

That same night the owner gave me a long talk about ladies, because of a complaint, and told me not to bother the perfume lady again. "Don't even think about her. Forget all about her. She's not right for you." Afterwards he took me to see some naked ladies. For relief, he said, when he stuffed some dollars in my pocket. I went into a room, I went into a lady, I came out of the silence lady, I came out of the empty room, I went back to my own room, I went to bed with the bottle of perfume, without sleeping, looking at light burning all night. The pretty perfume lady was in my heart's head more than ever.

That's the way it's always been, never seeing the woman persons who are in my heart's head again. Not my mother, or the pretty lady, or any of the other ladies. Just flower perfume in my bed to feel the patting. Patting makes a body feel good when it passes over your skin.

Patting. Patting.

I finally kept my name "the turtle," cause I always stayed inside my shell.

THE OLD MAN

> THE MOTHER *repeats the last word of some of the lines with a slight delay.*

Once, when I was visiting my brother
I had a dream.
Never forgotten.

I could see Pierre
like in real life, a grown man.
He got down on all fours in front of me.
He wanted to crawl inside me.
I was his skin and blood father.

So I helped him crawl inside my body.
I wanted him to be reborn.
I had a belly like a pregnant woman.
I wanted him.
Suddenly he came out of my mouth.
He was crying: "Here I come, Mama, here I come."
I spit him into a field.
Exactly where my father died.
And I shouted: "Pa, pa. Be reborn into the world.
Come back into the world. Come back to the world."

THE MOTHER falls silent.

From my bed, my eyes open, I could see the snow
everywhere.
A blue moon and the snow.
I thought, time is a whirlwind.
One day you're a son, next day you're a father.
One day you're a daughter, next day you're a mother.
And so on and so forth.
Through life and through death.

Scene 22

THE WITCH

THE MOTHER
My family that I hardly ever saw.
Once I saw them twice
in almost six months.
Except for my father the first time,
then except for my mother.
Because one died after the other.

The bishop said the mass for the dead.
Even him, he hardly spoke to me anymore.
The rest of the family
they're ashamed of me, you can see it.
I know, the family used to say they could see
madness in my eyes.

Like the witch in the sugarbush.
A woman who lived all alone
after her husband died
all alone down the road through the sugarbush.

Like the witch in the sugarbush.
I was the witch in the family
the witch in the convent
then the witch in the flat.

  She laughs.

To get away from them all.
I'd close my eyes
so I could talk to the jesuses inside.

The prayers had to be loud in my head
so the witch wouldn't look like me.
Never again.

No more letters, I mean nothing
from the mailman in my box
no news from the family.

My mother's dead.
The box is empty.
Always.
Even my brother the bishop
no news.

That was seven years after the mess.

The jesuses punish that far
punishment in your mailbox
so that silence rings in your ears.

The mother wished she could give birth
a second time to the child Pierre.
But the jesuses didn't want her to, I guess.

Miracles are something the jesuses save for heaven.

*She spits several times and goes back to lie on the
floor.*

I bought a painting.
Like when you do the stations of the cross.
A beautiful landscape.
It was a woman who did it.
How did she do it?

In silence.

Scene 23

DEPARTURES

THE OLD MAN
>We lived
>at different times.
>Pierre lives today.
>I live with yesterday.
>The son's mother always lived in the day before
>yesterday.
>We never arrived together
>in the same day.

>I'm going upstairs.
>If you're scared
>I'll come sleep downstairs.
>Tomorrow, Pierre, we'll go to the funeral.

THE MOTHER
>I feel relieved, now.
>It's all calmed down: my skin, my heart, my mind.
>I want to leave my body by myself
>my head held high.

>I want these moments to be mine alone.
>Like the times I'd leave the hotel
>with a catalogue lover
>breathing springtime
>pale yellow running through the branches.

>My head held high.

Yes, that's right, I'm leaving alone
my head held high.
I should be satisfied with that, I suppose.

> *THE MOTHER exits through the door which was left ajar. THE OLD MAN walks over to the door and brings in the other suitcases he'd left there.*

Scene 24

RETURN

THE SON has stuck his hands inside his shoes.

THE SON

I came to see that woman, my dead mother, a picture of the past lying in a bed with a door to hide her in the ground. I came by train. I never went back to the city. I took off my shoes. Today, I'm the one who lives here. Here.

Saguenay,
November 1989–October 1992